101 Money Saving Tips to Help Reduce Debt and Build Wealth

J. P. Conyers, Jr.

PUBLISHED BY:
J. P. Conyers, Jr.
Copyright © 2012

DISCLAIMER AND TERMS OF USE

No information contained in this book should be considered as physical, health related, financial, tax, or legal advice. Your reliance upon information and content obtained by you at or through this publication is solely at your own risk. The author assumes no liability or responsibly for damage or injury to you, other persons, or property arising from any use of any product, information, idea, or instruction contained in the content provided to you through this book.

Dedication

I would like to dedicate this book to the Millions of individuals and families that are suffering financially. The economy has decreased, more and more people are losing their jobs and most don't believe social security will be around for many more years. You may be in more debt than you have ever experienced and don't see an end in sight or a way to dig yourselves out of that debt.

I created this book to help individuals who want to conquer debt and take their lives back. In this book you will discover many different ways to find money to apply to your debt. I used most of these techniques to create a positive monthly savings in which I used to reduce my debt month after month.

I combined several of these money savings tips and the more I strategies I implemented the more money I was able to save. I started to save hundreds which I used to pay off debt. It snowballed and grew to saving thousands of dollars each and every month.

If you implement these ideas you should be able to have similar results depending on each individual's circumstances. I recommend taking your monthly savings these techniques can create and apply them towards your debts to snowball your monthly savings.

Forward

I have purposely created this book to be short in nature so it will be a quick read. I purposely made the cost very inexpensive so that anyone truly interested in taking back their lives can afford it.

There is no doubt in my mind the cost of this book can provide you with an ROI (return on invest) within your first month of implementing some of these techniques.

You will then want to take the ideas you feel will work for your specific situation and start implementing them to see some quick savings.

Once you get through the book you will probably start thinking of more and more ideas or ways you can come up with other money saving ideas of your own. Money saving can become addictive in nature once you see you have hope of getting out of debt.

If you have children it would be an ideal time to start teaching them about how to save money and make it a fun game. Have your children see who can come up with the most money saving ideas. This can teach your children that saving money can be just as much fun as spending it on toys.

It is reported that only 4% of the world's population is truly debt-free. With that being said, I knew there was a need to create this book, which can help individuals and families find enough money to start digging themselves out of debt once and for all.

It is sometimes strange to me why our education system doesn't teach individuals how to make money, save our money and live a debt free lifestyle. It is so simple once it is explained to you. I reiterate simple not always easy. I will be creating a book that will go into more detail on the techniques of getting anyone out of debt once and for all if they implement the techniques. For now I thought it would be better to get these money saving techniques in your hand so you can start coming up with more money each month to apply to your debts.

If you are one of the individuals that have conquered debt, you may want to employ some of these money-saving techniques to increase your monthly money savings plan.

My goal was to create a book that will truly make a difference in individuals lives that are buried in debt and do not see a way to break free. I too was once in this position, but implemented many of the strategies outlined in this book to a debt-free way of thinking and living.

My family and I were buried in so much debt. I never believed for a second that we would ever be free from debt or have any savings. I was determined to find a way out and started searching in all of our spending areas. My goal changed to purchasing things cheaper, to eliminating waste, limiting spending to only purchasing things that were needed.

I was able to locate several hundred dollars a month in savings to start applying it to my credit card with the least amount of debt. From there, as one bill was paid off I would then take the minimum amounts I was paying on that credit card and add it to the next bill with the least amount of debt. I continued the process until all unsecured debt was paid off. Once these credit cards were paid off it had increased my monthly savings into an amount in the thousands. I then started taking the thousands of dollars a month and applying it to our mortgage until it was also paid off.

I know this book is powerful if you implement decide to take action and implement its contents. If you are serious about finding money savings techniques then I'm sure you will find this book just what you are you looking for. I wish you all the best in your guest to finally achieve a debt free life.

Table of Contents

Save Money in a Trying Economy

Many people are asking, "How can I get out of debt in this economy?" The answer lies in this short, easy-to-implement book. Find out how to reduce your debt by cutting everyday costs and putting that money towards your debts. This book is going to give you 101 ideas to save your money as well as get your creative juices flowing so you can come up with your own ideas on how to save even more money.

Let's face it, with the economy in the tank, gas prices going through the roof, possibility of not having social security when you retire, pensions disappearing, you say what's a pension? Oh yea, that is what companies used to offer employees after they retired wherein they would give you a percentage of your yearly earnings for the rest of your life, usually in a monthly payment.

You see times have greatly changed and more and more financial responsibility lies on the individual. We have to start living under our own means so that we can save for the future, our kid's future, retirement and any other extra dreams you may have like traveling to Europe, sitting with your loved one at a café, sipping that espresso, and listening to the bell ring at the church in the center of town.

These dreams will be only a dream if we as individuals continue to live above our own means.
One thing this simple book will provide is 101 tips to help you immediately start saving money on purchases you are already making and move you into a mindset of saving money. Once you save the money, actually take the money and

put it into a separate bank account. This brings me to debt reduction principles that actually work.

Debt Reduction Principles That Actually Work

Pennies add up to dollars and dollars add up to multiple dollars. With a little time or once a month apply those savings to the smallest debt you have while maintaining your other minimum payments.

With time you will be applying the same principles that keep you enslaved to debt. In the beginning you will slowly reduce your debt, but this is where you don't want to give up and slip back into buying unnecessary items.

Once your first debt is paid off you now want to take that monthly payment and all the extra savings and now apply it to the next lowest balance.

For example,

Credit Card 1: Let's say you have a credit card debt with $5,000 and a minimum monthly payment of $500.

Credit Card 2: Has a credit card debt of $3,000 with a minimum monthly payment of $300.

Credit Card 3: Has a credit card debt of $1,000 with a minimum monthly payment of $100.

You would take your extra savings, for example purpose let's use a savings of $50 a month and apply it to the $1,000 credit card which would increase your payment to $150 dollars reducing the principle another $50.00 a month. You would only pay the minimum balance on the $5,000 and $3,000 credit cards. Once the $1,000 credit card is paid in full you would take the minimum payment ($100 + $50 = $150) along with the extra monthly saving and apply them to credit card debt 2.

So, for example purpose we would apply the $100 + $50 = $150 to credit card 2 along with the minimum payment of credit card 2. It would look like this $100 from minimum payment from credit card 3 (now paid off so the money is freed up) + $50 (extra savings) + $300 minimum credit card payment from credit card 2.

$100 +$50 + $300 = $450 a month applied to credit card 2.

So, now if we stick to our guns and don't add any new debt with the above example we would be able to pay off credit card 2 within 7 months. You would then do the same process for credit card 1 once credit card 2 is paid off.

$100 + $50 + $300 + $500 = $950 a month applied to credit card 1.

Now you are snow balling the debt and are reducing debt at a much faster rate than the beginning of our process. With the above example $5,000 / $950 a month payment you could have that credit card paid off in only 6 months.

Can you see the power behind taking those savings and compounding them in your favor to reduce debt? The process you are now implementing is the same process the unsecured debt is using against you, but you are now smarter and using compounding to your advantage to get out of debt.

Once smaller debts are erased, you can use the savings to reduce other debts like your home or save all the freed up money for retirement or your kid's college.

It is imperative that you decide not to incur any other debt so you can start the process of getting out of debt. It can be a smart decision to close your credit cards once the debt is eliminated to avoid having access to so much open credit. I would only keep your best credit card with the lowest rates open for a real emergency issue that may arise. Keeping one credit card open will also help you feel like you have a backup plan in a true emergency. I can't stress this enough though, **ONLY USE THE CREDIT CARD FOR EMERGENCYS!** Making un-necessary purchases again will cause your total debt reduction plan to be extended. Extending your debt elimination date can cause you to lose thousands of dollars in future investment dollars and delay being truly financially free. This leads me to the number one

reason people stay in debt called
Lack of Determination.

Lack of Determination

If you truly want to conquer debt and
become debt free you must have
determination to succeed or the tips
in this book on how to save money
won't help you. You have to have a
big enough **REASON! A WHY!**
Something that is more important to
you than staying in the vicious debt
cycle. Once you determine your
reason you will find more strength to
follow through and accomplish your
goal to become debt free.

I recommend sitting down in a quiet
place with your partner, if married, or
significant other and determine what
is your big enough reason to stay
focused until you achieve debt
freedom. If you don't find a strong
enough reason, you probably won't

follow through and this book will only add to your debt.

Every person is different and may have a different reason that burns deep inside them. It could be that you don't want to work until your 80 years old welcoming people to Wal-Mart. Don't get me wrong there is nothing wrong with type of job or working into your later years, but you may want to have the choice. You may want to provide for your kids college and know if you continue down the debt path you won't have enough to help them. You may want to have a better quality of living when retiring and traveling to your ideal secluded locations or taking the cruise of a lifetime.

If you determine that gut level, burning desire and make it a daily goal you can overcome the urge to spend excessively. You now have a more important goal, the goal to be financially debt free and that you are determined you are going to reach because you see an end in sight. You may only be months away from eliminating your debt and setting your life up for financial freedom. Only you can determine how far you want to go.

I will say this, and many others will agree saving money can become addictive. Once you start saving and see those debts being erased you will probably start thinking of other ways to save even more money or start a small no or low cost business that will produce even more money to help get out of debt even quicker.

The following are simple ideas that can help you save more money and if applied to your debts, can create a debt free lifestyle:

Saving Money on Food

Let's face it we all have to eat, right?
Well in the area of food, there is a lot
of room for savings. Grocery
shopping to eating out can take a big
chunk out of a person's budget. Here
are some great ideas for saving more
money in this area.

1.   A grocery store is not created
      equal. You can find everything
      from top priced grocery stores
      to discount grocery stores.
      Think about it, off brand
      grocery items are created
      somewhere right? Well a lot of
      the time the can goods are
      created at the same locations
      as those high priced can good
      distribution centers, but just
      have the labels changed. The
      food is still the same quality but
      the price can be greatly

reduced due to less overhead and marketing.

2.	Find a discount shopping network like Sam's or Costco. They offer lower prices when you buy in bulk. If your family consumes a lot of a specific type of food, it may save a lot if you buy those items in bulk. Example: Cereal, if your family consumes a lot of cereal you may want to look at the savings of buying cereal in bulk. Other examples would be toilet paper, paper towels, dog food, dog treats, coffee, produce, milk, eggs etc.

3.	Never go to the grocery store when you're hungry. It is proven that if you're hungry, you tend to purchase more unneeded items you may not have purchased if you weren't hungry. Let's face it, everything sounds good when we're hungry and we tend to overspend when we are shopping while hungry.

4.   Make a list before shopping. You can save a lot of money by only purchasing grocery items that are needed and on your list. If it's not on your list don't buy it. Grocery stores place some of the highest priced items eye level for kids and impulse purchases close to the cash register, hoping you'll see it and grab those last minute items at the register.

5.   Watch for your local grocery store flyers. Take each flyer and compare the specials for that week. You may have to go to more stores but can reduce your food bill by buying the items needed on sale.

6.   Stock up on the sale items while they are discounted. Try and buy a month or two's worth of these products.

7.   Compare the unit price of items to similar items to determine the lowest price.

8.   Fruits and Vegetables can become expensive. Purchase your fruits and vegetables in season for the lowest price. I know blueberries are very expensive in off season. When the blueberries are in season the price drops and they provide you with a larger quantity. You may also want to look at purchasing frozen fruits that are sometimes cheaper than fresh fruits.

9.   Ask for a rain check if the sales items are sold out so you can save money when they get

more in stock.

10. Most grocery stores have a discount isle for slightly damaged goods. Always look in this isle for items on your list.

11. Stay away from boxed and convenience foods. These items are more expensive than foods you can cook. Shopping the outer isles of the store can provide the healthiest foods which tend to also be cheaper. Shopping the inner isles are where the higher price, less healthy boxed meals are located.

12. Purchase your non-food items at discount retail store like Sam's, Costco, Wal-Mart, Target etc. They are usually cheaper than purchasing them at the grocery store.

13. Look for a local butcher shop to purchase your meat. Local butchers often offer lower prices than retail chain grocery stores and some offer meat raised in your local area. Healthier meats come from free-range farms and that aren't feed corn or injected with hormones. They are allowed to graze on the grass and tend to have less stress making the meat much healthier.

14. Locate a local cattle farmer and go in with a friend to purchase a half of cow. You can decide how you want to the cow processed for your meat needs. You can pick ground beef, roast, steak etc. You may need an extra freezer to store the cow but there is huge savings in this tip.

15. Locate a local pig farmer and

purchase 1 or 2 pigs. You can have the pig made into whatever types of meat you enjoy such as sausage, bacon or ham.

16.   Once you locate a grocery store, inquire about a loyalty discount program that can save you money. The loyalty discount program can provide additional discounts when shopping at that store.

17.   Keeping track of prices from the different stores can help you determine a bargain when you see it.

18.   If you're lucky to have a farmers market or roadside stand, stop by one to pick up fresh fruits and vegetables. The prices are usually lower and you can negotiate a cheaper price. It may help if you

become a regular before attempted a discounted price.

19.   Be sure to ask your store if they run any specials on certain days like Thursday is double coupon day, or specials on day old bread etc. and plan you're shopping around this day.

20.   Figure out a grocery budget and stick to it. If your family is fed easily on $200 a week, don't spend a penny more. Stay within the budget you set.

21.   Once you have your budget amount, take that amount out of your bank account and save it in an envelope as cash. Now only buy groceries with your cash envelope. Plan your purchases to get the most meals with your grocery budget. When the money is gone for the week stop buying.

22. When purchasing chicken, purchase the chicken with the skin still on it. Skinless chicken is almost always more due to them removing the skin.

23. Save money by purchasing deli meats and cheeses from the dairy case instead of the deli. The deli prices tend to be higher than the dairy case.

24. Look for in store coupons. While shopping, some grocery stores have coupons for certain items sticking out from the shelves. Simply pick a coupon up while selecting the items.

25. Store check outs may not always be accurately scanning your sale items. Watch the register while your items are being rung up to avoid overpaying for an item.

26. Now that you purchased your items check the receipt before leaving and make sure all coupons were applied correctly along with sale items.

Saving With Coupons

Coupons are a great way to save a lot of money over the course of a year. Staying dedicated to clipping them and using them every time you shop can add up to some great savings.

27. Sign up to a coupon club or newsletter. They will usually send coupons to you via email once or twice a month depending on the company. You can simply search "Coupons" in your search bar and come up with thousands of

website that offer free coupons on groceries, clothing, dinning out, and just about anything you can think of.

28. Start a coupon swap with friends and family members. Swap coupons you don't use with coupons you do use.

29. Check with your grocery store to find out if they have specific days for double or triple coupon days. Shop accordingly.

30. When you enter the store always check there in store coupon magazine. There are coupons in there that aren't always in the weekly sales flyer.

31. Contact all manufactures that you purchase products from and inquire if they have a coupon program. If so, asked to be put on their mailing or

email list for additional coupons.

32.　Check and see if your community has local coupon mailers and get on their lists. There are usually several good coupons inside one mailer.

33.　Try and save your coupons and use them when your items you purchase go on sale to get a super saver discount.

34.　Use a coupon organizer to achieve the best results with coupons. Staying organized and using the coupons before they expire will save you money.

Extreme couponing has become so popular that there is now a show about it. Some of those individuals get so good they purchase over a thousand dollars of groceries for a small fee or some can zero out the register. If you want to become this good with couponing I want you to know it takes some time and preparation finding the coupons, clipping them, organizing them which could take several hours a week to accomplish. It could become a part-time job, but if you have the time this could save you hundreds to thousands of dollars per month.

Saving Money by Eating At Home

Eating at home is another great way to save money. Why is it cheaper to eat at home? The greatest cost when we eat out is that someone else is preparing our meals and they get a premium price for that service. So, when you do the prep work and cook your meals yourself, you save that cost. Remember you can also eat a much healthier meal when you make it yourself.

35.   Eating at home can save a lot of money over the course of a year. Let's face it, it's much easier to pick something up while you're out and not have to cook, no prep time, just eat and pay. Well you're losing a lot of your budget if you're eating out very much.

36.   Cook meals ahead for the week. This will save time and have home cooked meals easily accessible. Meals can quickly be ready to eat while saving money.

37.   Gather several recipes that afford you quick, easily prepared meals. This can keep you out of the drive thru and more money in your pocket.

38. Most families have their
     pantries filled with items. Try
     not shopping for a week and
     eat whatever you have in your
     pantry. Take the grocery
     shopping money for that week
     and put it in your savings
     account. Big savings.

39. Bringing your lunch to work can
     really add up to some great
     savings. If you eat out every
     day that can get expensive. By
     bringing your already prepared
     meals you may save as much
     as $5.00-$10.00 a day and eat
     a healthier meal.

40. When shopping in discount,
     wholesale clubs be sure to pick
     up some snack foods you enjoy.
     Add these to your lunch bag so
     you can avoid overpaying at the
     vending machine.

41. Clean out your Freezer by

eating what's in it. You can cut your grocery bill again by eating up the freezer food before it gets freezer burn and you have to throw it out.

42. Make one day a week pick it night. Combine all the leftovers and pick out separate meals for the family. This way you will not have to throw away any food and you will have gotten the biggest bang for your buck.

43. For other snack ideas, buy chips and pretzels in bigger bags and bring some of your favorite's snacks in a zip lock bag. Definitely cheaper than the vending machine.

44. Create a soup and salad night or a vegetarian casserole night to cut down on the expensive meat purchases.

45.   If you enjoy gardening, plant your own tomatoes, cucumbers, lettuce, corn, etc. to save even more on your grocery bill. You'll have organic grown produce you grew without the harmful pesticides. You may even have fun watching over your garden.

46.   Instead of buying an expensive cup of coffee on your drive to work, you can usually purchase your favorite coffee at your discount club for way less. Simply brew your own Starbuck, Dunkin Donuts, etc. from home. This one tip alone can save a lot of money in just one week.

47.   If you're really thrifty you can mix your favorite premium coffee with regular coffee. Simply mix the premium coffee 3 parts to 1 part regular coffee.

This will make the premium coffee go even further without a loss of flavor.

48.   Stock up on your favorite ice cream or frozen treat instead of buying ice cream from the ice cream truck. You'll always have your children's favorite treat on hand when they hear the ice cream man, but you're saving money while giving them what they want.

49.   Create some meals from scratch when possible. These meals are not only healthier but much cheaper than drive thru meals and convenient box meals.

50.   Purchase a bread machine and make your own healthy bread from scratch without the unwanted added ingredients from store bought bread. Your

house will smell so good.

51. If your fruits start to expire, get creative and make banana bread, or a strawberry desert cup. The idea here is to not have any waste. Consume everything you purchase. This will save you money over time.

52. The same goes for your vegetables. If they start to expire make a soup or cut them up for a salad that night. If you think creative and consume all foods you purchase you will get more bang for your shopping dollar. No waste and more meals equal savings.

53. Here's a great tip if you feel crafty. My grandma always used to can her fruits and vegetables. It can be a little time consuming but can be a fun, low cost hobby that saves

you money.

54. Buying popcorn in bulk and popping it yourself can save you money instead of buying the bagged popcorn that is already prepared. Have you ever read the label of what's in there? Natural ingredients like popcorn, oil, butter and salt is all you need to have some great tasting popcorn while saving money.

Saving Money When Eating Out

If you do decide to eat out you can save money with coupons or limit what you select to eat and drink. You can save money on drinks, deserts and sharing entrees. Everyone needs a break now and then but by limiting the amount of times you choose to eat out can also give you some great savings.

55.   If you choose to eat out you
       can save money by eating out
       at breakfast and lunch. Dinner
       prices tend to be higher in price
       than similar lunch meals.

56.   If eating out is something you
       enjoy, try and cut back on the
       amount of times per month you
       choose to eat out and make it a
       special occasion. For example if
       you eat out every Friday night,
       try eating out once a month as
       a reward for saving the extra
       money.

57.   When eating out try to locate a
       coupon for buy and entrée get
       the second one free. Or locate
       a 25-50% off coupon of the
       total bill or other promotional
       specials.

58.   When eating out ask your

waiter/waitress if they have any specials of the day. Some restaurants provide excellent meals at a discounted price.

59.   Ask your favorite restaurant if they have offers for a free birthday meal and sign up. What a way to celebrate your birthday, a free meal while saving money.

60.   Most restaurants have increased the size of their meals giving the individual value. Try sharing an entrée. With the meals being so large most people can't finish their entire entrée anyway and have to bring some home. This is a way to not break the bank and still enjoy eating out.

61.   Try eating out during a week night instead of the weekend when the prices tend to be

higher.

62.   Try to avoid drinking costly soda and alcohol while eating out. This one tip can add up quickly for a family of 4. If soda is $1.50 a glass and you order 4 sodas you just saved $6.00 off your bill in drinks. Needless to say you probably save even more on alcohol.

63.   When eating out avoid desserts. Have your favorite dessert waiting for you when you get home and give your stomach some time to settle. Restaurants tend to be highly priced for what you get. If you must have a dessert there, then try splitting it. This alone can cut your dessert bill in half.

64.   If you decide you are going to eat out try and locate a discount restaurant coupon

book. Most coupon books have coupons that offer half off dinning or buy and entrée and get the second one free or half off.

65.   If you are eating out for business purposes speak with your accountant to get the proper deductions come tax time. This can add up over a full year.

66.   Always check your bill before you pay to catch any errors that the waiter/waitress may not be aware of.

Saving Money with Your Home

Your home is a great asset. There are many tips you may not have thought of when trying to save money. Below are some great tips for saving money at your home.

67. Speak with a loan officer about refinancing your home. With today's mortgage rates being so low, you can save thousands of dollars over the course of years with just a drop in interest rate of 1-2%.

68. Putting a little extra money towards your homes principle each month can have you paying your home off early and saving thousands of dollars in interest.

69. Make sure to cancel Private Mortgage Insurance or PMI after paying your mortgage

down 20%. It may be required until you have at least 20% equity in your home. They may not automatically remove the PMI insurance so it is best for you to contact your mortgage company and request that it be removed once you reach their cut off limit. PMI insurance is only in place to benefit the loan owners from default payments, not to help you recover any money, so get this off as soon as you possibly can.

70. If you are a single home owner find a roommate that can pay you rent and maybe some of the utilities. This can really reduce your monthly expenses.

71. When in your home turn your thermostat up a few degrees in the hot summer months and down a few degrees in the winter months. Heating and

cooling bills can greatly be reduced by simply implementing this tip. It's cheaper to run a ceiling fan in the summer because it draws less electricity. In the winter put more clothes on to stay warm while lowering the thermostat.

72. Saving on other Electricity. Turn off all unnecessary electrical devices when there not needed. Example, turn off lights that are not needed. Turn off porch lights if not needed. Turn Televisions off if no one is watching them. If you need noise in the room a radio is much cheaper to run than your television.

73. Make sure water pipes and toilets are not leaking. If water constantly runs your water meter doesn't stop either.

Leaking pipes and toilets can greatly increase your bill.

74.   Find a local handyman you can call when things break down in your home. Handymen charge less than a professional licensed contractor but can fix many problems not requiring a licensed contractor. You can find excellent handyman that come recommended by companies like Angie's List.

75.   Get quotes for your insurance needs. Shopping for insurance can save you hundreds a month by getting special discounts some insurance companies offer that others don't.

76.   Mortgage Life Protection insurance offered by mortgage companies can sometimes be expensive. Instead consider purchasing a Term life

insurance policy that covers your mortgage balance in case something happens to you. This may give you the most coverage at the cheapest price. Always shop insurance policies and consult with a trusted insurance professional to see your best options at the cheapest prices.

77.   Compare the saving if you increase your deductibles. You may find some savings by simply increasing the amount of your deductible. Each person is different and you should always pick a deductible you are comfortable with.

Stop the Leaking Money by Purchasing For Needs Not Wants

When setting up a budget you will want to review your bank account.

49

Looking at your bank account and locate any unnecessary purchases. You have to be honest with yourself here. If you're stopping for a coffee every morning, is that a necessity or a want. Separate your needs from your wants. These are the purchases you can eliminate. I'm not taking about eliminating them forever, but just until you get out of debt. Once you're out of debt you can afford to buy anything you want without carrying all that debt around on your shoulders.

78.   Create a budget and stay firm with your commitment. Setting a budget and sticking to it can save hundreds of dollars a month in savings.

79.   Look at your bank statements to see where you are spending your money. Take a blank piece of paper and make two

columns. One column for needed and the other not needed. Now go through your bank statement and put the expenses in the following two columns, needed or not needed. Now look at all the non-needed expenses that can be cut for additional savings.

80. Try eliminating cash expenses. Limit the amount of cash you carry with you to avoid impulse purchases. Use your bank card when purchases are absolutely necessary. It is easier to spend cash for non-needed items than if you were to put those items on your bank debit card. Keeping less cash on you and switching to your bank card for your purchases will help to cut down on the non-needed items purchased.

81. Using your bank card for

purchases should cut down on costly cash withdrawals from ATM machines.

82. Consolidate your credit cards to your lowest interest rate cards then follow the above plan for getting out of debt. Ask for a no fee transfer, some credit card will transfer balances for no fees to increase the amount on their card in hopes you won't pay off your card for a long time, increasing their profit with interest payments and late fees. This can save you a lot of money in interest payments each month. Apply the savings to the credit card with the lowest amount.

83. Make it a goal to study financial and money management principles. The more you learn about these principles and apply them to your savings plan

the faster you can achieve
financial freedom from debt.

84. Contact an attorney in your
     area for proper estate planning.
     You want as much of your hard
     earned dollars to stay with your
     loved ones in the event of an
     unexpected illness or death.

85. Contact an Investment broker
     to learn more about your
     investment options once your
     debts are paid off and you have
     extra money to invest. Safe
     investments can really increase
     your overall worth.

Saving Money Miscellaneous Ways

Here are some miscellaneous ways to
help you save even more money.
You may even want to start a small
business to help create some extra

income to wipe out that debt even faster.

86.   If you need a baby sitter, look to your family and friends first. One of your friends or family members may need to make extra money and give you a discounted price from the high price of daycare centers.

87.   If you are paying someone to cut your grass, find time and do it yourself. Individuals are paying $25-$40 to have an average size yard mowed. That's a savings of $100-$160 a month minus your own gas and lawn mower upkeep.

88.   Think of starting your own small low cost, no cost side business. If you have a skill, knowledge or hobby in a particular area why not put it to use and make another income.

Brainstorm some ideas like babysitting, lawn mower repair, mowing yards, power washing, painting houses or apartments on the weekend, tiling business, mobile car washing business, typing papers for college student, starting an online business, the list goes on and on. Just let your imagination take over and brainstorm all your ideas. Then ask your family and friends what they think would be good a side job for you. They may think of ideas you didn't.

89.   If you're planning a vacation contact a travel agent. Tell them what type of vacation you would like to take. Example, a tropical vacation. Your travel agent may be able to locate trips to locations you didn't think of at discounted rates. Your travel agent may also find

an off peak time for you to travel for the cheapest price while still enjoying the same vacation. Simply plan your vacation around the non-peak season. It probably will be less crowded and more enjoyable.

90.   Beauty schools are a great place to get the whole families haircut and styled. Beauty schools charge a discounted price since your stylist is still in the learning process. Don't worry, there is a teacher there guiding the student so you don't leave with a lop-sided haircut. This is an excellent way to save money that most people don't think about.

91.   Pre-plan meals that involve the oven. Your oven takes time to pre heat and that cost money. If you can have several meals prepped ahead of time and

ready to bake one after the other, you won't have to use your oven as much during the week, thus cutting down on excessive gas or electric usage.

92.   The same principle applies when drying your clothes. If you can wash several loads of laundry and wait to dry them one load after the other you'll save money. Once the first load is dried your dryer will be warm which will help dry the other loads quicker saving you money.

93.   Have a regular maintenance schedule for your vehicle and home. A regular maintenance schedule for your car can keep it in peak performance and help it last longer. Your furnace and air conditioning unit should also be maintained for peak performance saving you more

on your heating and cooling bill.

94.   The next time you need to
      replace your carpet research
      getting a thicker pad under
      your carpet with a middle grade
      carpet. When you walk on the
      carpet you notice a much nicer,
      softer feel while saving money
      on carpet.

95.   Going to replace your furniture.
      Shop discount furniture stores
      like Weekends Only. They offer
      some great savings while
      providing quality furniture.

96.   Ask your local drug store if they
      offer rebate programs. Many
      items will end up being free or
      next to free.

97.   Be determined to avoid impulse
      purchases. If you notice you
      purchase items on impulse at
      the mall then avoid going to the

mall unless you have a specific item you <u>NEED</u> to purchase. These impulse purchases can deeply cut into a budget and wreak havoc on your savings. Impulse buying must be addressed if you are going to save money and get out of debt.

98.   A great place to pick up items you may need is at garage sales. Certain items can be found in great shape and only cost a nickel to a few dollars. Garage sales offer everything from tools, kitchen items, couches, paintings, kid's clothes and everything is usually at very cheap prices. You might even have a great time trying to find the next bargain on your list. Bottom line, garage sales can save you a lot of money.

99.   Shop for your families

Christmas and birthday gifts when there on sale. Why wait and pay full price? Think ahead and be on the lookout for items you know your family would love for their Christmas and/or birthday gifts.

100. When renting movies rent from kiosks. You can rent a movie for just a dollar. Most kiosks movie rental companies will also offer incentives by providing you a free movie code once in a while or discount codes to rent two movies and get the third one free. If you rent from a movie rental store you probably are paying four dollars for the same movie. Renting from a kiosk can save you 400%. This can really add up over the course of a year. Another great way to save if you're a movie buff and are looking for cheap entertainment

is using Netflix. At the time of this writing Netflix offers unlimited, steaming movies and television shows for only $8.00 a month. If you rent more than 8 movies a month you're saving money. A monthly payment will also help you budget and know you will only be spending $8.00 a month.

101. You can save thousands of dollars on this last way to save money. Look at purchasing a used vehicle from a reputable dealer. New cars quickly depreciate and continue to depreciate over the next few years. Look for a vehicle approximately two to three years old with low mileage. You will save thousands of dollars from the vehicles original price, letting the first owner absorb those first few years of depreciation. You will

get a vehicle that has low
mileage and a nice look for a
greatly reduced price. WOW
what a savings.

Conclusion

This book was created for individuals that can't seem to find any extra money and are hurting financially. Most families that implement these simple saving strategies can save hundreds to thousands of dollars a year.

This book is a simple system, and if implemented will help you get started on saving money right away. There are 101 ideas to kick start your savings plan. Hopefully this book will spark something deep inside you to see the endless possibilities for savings.

We all have options put before us each and every day. Do you have a strong enough why a strong enough reason to take over your financial life.

Dig deep, do some soul searching. Don't put off this part of the plan. I'm sure you've heard the saying **_"You don't plan to fail, you simply fail to plan!"_** (Writer Unknown).

Don't wake up looking to retire and be buried in debt. If you don't take action now, then when will you? Carpi Diem (seize the day). If you want to ever get out of debt and become financially free you have to eliminate debt. The sooner you start your plan the sooner you can get out of debt and start saving for retirement or other personal desires.

None of us wake up and plan to fail we just get busy and tell ourselves we are going to start saving some day in the near future. Well I'm here to tell you that every day you fail to plan you are losing out on money you could be saving for your future.

Debt is expensive and causes so much pain and anxiety in individuals and families' lives. Banks and credit card companies are the ones making the money. They love to offer low minimum payments because each month they are making millions of dollars. They love for you to pay only the minimum, it keeps you paying them interest, which is pure, profit every month you make a payment.

If you stay on their minimum payment plan you can plan on paying that debt for years and that's without putting any additional purchases on your credit card. Paying for items this way can cost you hundreds if not thousands of extra dollars over you're original purchase price.

The key is thinking a little differently and finding where the money is leaking out of your savings and then fill the holes. The faster you fill the holes and use the new found savings to pay down your debts, the quicker you can start to accumulate wealth.

If you are serious about getting out of debt please find your why. If you have a family, sit down and talk about making a plan that everyone can agree on and implement it together.

Bringing your family together and agreeing on the program can really build a great support group for when times get tough. Support each other, make saving money fun and see who can save the most from their own ideas. When you make it fun it becomes enjoyable.

If you aren't really wanting to save money and it becomes a chore, well, you probably will not follow the program very long, give up and go right back to spending more than your making, growing your debt bigger and bigger.

Let's think through that for a minute. In a few more years is it going to be harder or easier to get out of the hole? Harder right? So, today is the first day of the rest of your life.

Your future is in your hands. It may seem like a daunting task right now, but if you implement this simple program you will shortly see how much money you can save and apply to your debts.

So guys please, please, please find your why. Sit down and brainstorm ideas to save money, put this books savings plan to use. Get with your loved ones to share more ideas. Then above all take action!! Put your plan into an actionable plan. Start your plan today and don't wait until tomorrow because it will be costing a lot more money in the long run.

I truly want you to become successful and enjoy a debt free life. It just takes determination that you will be one of the few who dedicate themselves to taking action. If you take action on these principles you will succeed.

Saving When Debt Free

If you are already debt free, I would like to applaud you. You are in a small percentage of people in the United States. You have found your why, your reason and have been disciplined to accomplish the task of becoming debt free.

If you are already debt free, please use the ideas in this book to compound your savings. It may spark new ideas for you save even more money per month adding more money to your net worth.

One of my financial advisers once told me it was easier to hold on to the money you have already made than it is to make more. This theory still holds true, especially in this economy.

Another little comment is what changed my life. I never thought about money like this before. He stated, "If you spend everything you make your still broke."

He gave me a couple of made up scenarios and then hit me with this:

If medical doctor X makes $200,000 dollars a year and his/her bills consume all the money they make, they are still broke. They may have fancier toys and homes but if their net worth is $0.00, their still BROKE!

There are also individuals that make a modest living making $40,000 household income but have saved money and live a debt free life style with $400,000 in investments. So, in this scenario who is the person with the most wealth?

He went on to say it is not how much money you make but how much money you save and invest wisely that will give you a secure future. So, no matter the amount of money you make, you need to live below your means in order to save for the future.

I left his office kind of in shock, but his words rang true to my spirit. I saw something that day that opened my eyes and learned that anyone can become financially independent if they truly wanted to. I figured out quickly that day, the choice lies within each of us.

Hopefully this book can help you take your financial future back into your control and not the big credit card companies, mortgage companies and businesses.

I hope you enjoyed this book and that it has sparked something deep inside you to take action and make the necessary changes to start saving your hard earned money.

I know the content of this book has changed my future. It has given me and many others a feeling of true freedom. Remember true freedom comes from owning your life and not being indebted to others.

Once you accomplish a debt free style of living, you truly will be one of the top 4% of the people in the world and will have accomplished something that most people only dream about. I can't tell you enough how liberating a debt free life can be. To wake up in the morning and feel that a pressure is gone, the stress lifted, and knowing now you can invest for your future.

I am working on my next book, which will be going into more details on how to use your new found money savings to help eliminate your debts. In my next book, I will cover tips and techniques that I have used to accelerate my debt reduction in the fastest amount of time. I truly want to provide value and want to work with individuals that are looking for a better way of life than to be indebted. I want for you what I now have in my life, freedom.

Once again I'd like to thank you for your purchase of this book. I hope you enjoyed it and it has opened your eyes to how important it is to save money and get out of debt. The decision lies inside each and every individual. Find your why and take action, you'll thank yourself once you did.

I was devastated when my debt grew to over six figures. Our real estate investments tanked, business expenses were put on our credit cards and we started sinking fast.

Two short sales, a bankruptcy, and several years of stress took its toll on me and my family's lives.

I started formulating a debt elimination plan that is still in full force today. My family has paid off all debts minus our mortgage, which is quickly diminishing.

I wish I would have only known then what I know now, who knows how much quicker we could have been debt free and building wealth for our future.

I know how much our family was hurting while we were in debt, how little extra money there was at the end of the month. We were struggling to find enough money to provide for our family's needs.

I decided it was my new passion to get out of debt and build wealth. If my techniques worked for my family, I knew they would work for others.

I couldn't sit by with critical information that could help others take back their lives and financial futures.

So, I decided to write a book that lays out the very simple techniques we used to become debt free from credit cards, car loans, and eventually our home.

In the book you will learn how to pay off your debts including your mortgage in just a handful of years. I discovered by simple math that this is the fastest way to reduce debts and build wealth.

You'll be surprised to learn why it's not your fault you're in debt.

Why continuing to pay off your mortgage early and before starting to invest can leave you with more than a million dollars in the same time period.

Let's face it guys; we are not taught in school or anywhere else how to take financial responsibility and achieve financial prosperity.

You'll also discover why those marketing tricks, such as "low, easy to afford monthly payments" or "limited quantities, be sure and purchase today before supplies run out" are just great marketers stealing your financial future.

The program had to be easy for me to follow in order to stick with it. There is no real "Budget" if you will, to follow. Just a little education combined with a simple to follow plan that is actionable. That's it!

I'm sure that anyone who truly wants to eliminate debt and build wealth can do it. You do have to take action and be determined for a handful of years to totally eliminate your debts.

If this sounds like something you're struggling with go now to Amazon and purchase a copy of my book.

My book's name is ***"Debt Elimination – The Ultimate Guide to Financial Prosperity"*** ***(Financial Prosperity Series).***

My book has everything in it you will need to become debt free. I want to be honest with you, it is a simple to implement plan that requires action. You must decide to take action, stay motivated and apply the techniques to receive the results your desire.

If you decide to purchase any of my books and feel you received value, could I ask you a big favor? Would you do me a favor and go back to by book in Amazon Kindle or Amazon for physical books and leave me a positive review.

It is truly my goal to provide value for individuals that purchase my books. If you feel like my books have provided value I would appreciate you leaving some valuable, positive feedback on my Amazon book page.

Your review may be the deciding factor that helps someone else that needs help, decide to purchase my books and give them a better quality of life.

Thank you again for putting your faith in me and my books.

I would like to wish you all the best in your lives and tell you that I believe in you. Stay dedicated to your goals and a debt reduction program and you will achieve your financial dreams.

My true goal in life is to help people change their lives for the better, one person at a time.

I wish you all the best. Here's to your success!

J. P. Conyers, Jr.